NO MATTER
What

Choose JOY whether you stay in
or leave a hard marriage

By **CORAL WARD**

with insights from

Jamee Andelin

TABLE OF CONTENTS

INTRODUCTION

The day after Andy left, I had the craziest prompting from above that I needed to share my journey with the world—the journey that enabled me to find joy through all the hard. It was an internal struggle. *Who was I to write a book?* My grammar and eloquence with wording are definitely not my strengths. Yet here I am.

I longed to be true to myself, have hope, and live my faith while I was in a hard marriage. I knew I wanted to fight for the marriage I signed up for, so I did. I fought hard, and I fought for many years. Later, I committed to be true to myself and God while getting divorced. I found that being true to myself while in a hard marriage and being true to myself while getting divorced weren't so different after all.

I am not a marriage expert, but I am your friend, Coral, and I want to share with you tools and ideas that took me years to discover as I dug deep and found inner joy while staying in a challenging marriage.

In this book, my goal is not just to throw you a life preserver as you tread through tough waters, but to help you build a beautiful boat. We will navigate these waters together by exploring emotions, morals, boundaries, children, and ways you can create your own roadmap as you fight for *you*.

At the end of each chapter, I have a secret weapon to help you through this storm. Jamee Andelin is a Certified

Life Coach who has helped hundreds of individuals and couples to heal their marriages and live with no regrets. Jamee has been my personal marriage and life coach. She will be asking you some of the thought-provoking questions she asked me, and she will also include helpful insights that have empowered me to define who I am and how I want to show up with the courage I so desperately need.

Coaching was a different experience for me than having a counselor. I love that I had both, because both helped me see the value and the change that I personally needed. Through counseling, I dug deep into my emotions, my challenges, my past … and through life coaching, I worked mostly on my thought process and what I wanted to feel and accomplish in my life and marriage.

The principles shared throughout this book have taken me a lifetime to learn. As you read each chapter, ask yourself, "What am I hearing beyond what Coral has written?" This is when your deep-rooted, self-learning process happens. This is where you will feel guided and supported. My intention is to help you look for the answers and the hope you need not just inside my story, but inside of YOU.

My choices, my journey, and my outcome are and will always be mine. Your journey will look different. Just because my marriage ended in divorce does not mean that this is how your marriage will or should end. The message I want to shout from the rooftops is that you can be true to yourself, find the joy in your life, and come to a place where you can honestly believe that you are living with no regrets!

This book has a unique format. I am breaking a lot of author rules here, but I want to share with you exactly what I feel can bless your life in the most impactful way. With that being said, you will find in the first chapter my story, who I am, and what makes me — ME. Chapter one is in chronological order to help you understand what kind of life I have lived in my thirty-eight years. All of the subsequent chapters are a bit different. Each chapter has a topic and a theme that has helped to save me... even when I have felt fifteen feet underwater. These chapters are not in chronological order — on purpose. They were written as they came to my heart in deciding what principles and insights have helped me both while in my hard marriage and after my divorce. These are the very tools and strategies that have saved me and continue to save me as I venture on to new uncharted territories of life.

I wrote all of this with the intent to help you realize that you can find joy *no matter what* your circumstance is — *no matter what* you choose, and in some cases, what has been chosen for you. With the right tools, habits, and resources, you get to decide how you show up for yourself, even when you feel you are in the eye of the storm and there is no safe way out.

Friend, you are incredible.
You can do hard things. You can find joy in the

No Matter What!

Chapter 1

A GIRL'S GOTTA DREAM

I'm a California girl named after my great-great-grandmother Coral McDade. I claim to be five-foot-three when I give my hair a little more volume on top. I have blue eyes, blonde hair (well, my girl Katie helps keep me blonde), and have always believed I was born to do great things.

As a six-year-old, I pondered what those great things might be as my dirty, bare feet nearly touched the sky. I pumped the swing hanging from Grandma and Grandad's giant oak tree, replaying my grandmother's words of encouragement: *Coral, God loves you, and He can help you be your best and happiest self.*

Rays of warm sunshine fell over me as this truth sunk deep. I knew I was going to take on the world while finding my Prince Charming and that I would never have to experience the hard times my single mom endured. I was going to find someone just like my grandfather: strong, smart, funny, tall, dark, and handsome!

I pulled back on the swing, let my strawberry-blonde hair fly out behind me, and decided one thing for sure: I would never end up making choices like Dad had made. We lost so much because of his bad choices. *Could I use his life as an example of what not to do?* I wondered. I thought of my fourteen siblings in our enormous, blended family, and I knew I could get away with whatever I wanted because there were so many of us. But the memory of Dad's choices made my gut twist with sadness. No, I would not be the kid who tried to get away with everything. I would stand strong and choose the right.

I didn't know all the choices standing strong would lead to, like serving a mission for my church at Temple Square in Salt Lake City. But I knew in my heart that I would always follow God and be a good Christian girl.

As the breeze and summer sun embraced me, I pumped my swing even higher, and a dream materialized. In my dream, I would one day find a good Christian boy and live happily ever after.

On May 24, 2008, my dream came true! I was twenty-four years old when I found my Prince Charming. He was tall, dark, and handsome, and we had so much fun together. We dated six months, got engaged, and six months after that, we were married! We had a fabulous relationship, and our five-hundred-square-foot apartment on the third floor was perfect. Other than hauling groceries up three flights of stairs, I was living the dream!

But What Happens When the Dream Is a Nightmare?

Three years later, I sat pregnant in a church pew with my arms around our two children, ages one and two. The speaker's lips were moving, but I didn't hear him. I only felt the disappointment that sat in my gut like a stone—a stone I had been trying to ignore.

When Andy slid into the pew beside me twenty minutes later, the stone expanded. I didn't mind him being late; the problem was that he didn't want to be there. In truth, I didn't want to be there either. For the first time in my life, I didn't want to be at church. Could I really hide the pain and suffering from everyone? I felt like our home was made of glass and our dysfunction was on display for the whole congregation. Could they see right through me? Did they know that our family was hanging on by a thread that was about to snap?

Glancing around at the seemingly perfect families, I wondered if it would be better if they did know. If I had a single person to confide in, I might not feel so alone. If only I could say the words out loud to someone who cared, I might know what to do. But what would I even say? How could I wrap words around the fact that after three years of wholeheartedly believing in our marriage, I had come to a rude awakening.

My husband had struggles that could tear our marriage to pieces. This crisis swallowed me whole. Seemed to break me beyond repair. I felt as though I was being lifted up by a massive hurricane—spun around 7,236 times and spit out in the middle of the sea. And here, in a room full of people, I was drowning alone.

Our two-year-old started to squirm, and I handed him to Andy. *How ironic,* I thought, *that even though Andy and I grew up in the same faith, the gap between our values was as massive as the Grand Canyon.*

Had I made the wrong choice?

When I prayed about marrying him, did I not pray with enough intent?

How could God let this happen to me?

What did I do to deserve this?

All of these questions cycled through my mind 3,544 times a day.

What do I do now?

Do I stay or do I go?

Does every marriage have this many problems?

I mean, what happened to my fairy-tale love story?

It was hard to function most days. I went from feeling hopeful to doubting and questioning everything I had ever done and every choice I had ever made.

A few months later, driving home from the carpool through sheets of rain, I poured my heart out to God. "Heavenly Father, I can't do this on my own. I need help. I don't know who to turn to." The image of Mom popped into my mind, but I couldn't bear the thought of adding to her burden. "I don't want to get my family involved. They would have a biased opinion anyway," I told Him.

Using my sleeve to wipe away a few tears and my runny nose, I continued, "I love my friends, Heavenly Father, but if I complain to them, they will just see the bad. They will resent Andy instead of seeing the full picture of all the good times. Andy was good to me. He loved me. But I just can't live like this. Please," I choked out, "help me help myself. I just feel so alone."

Where to Turn? Reaching Out for Help

Counselors and therapists seemed like the best place to start, so one sunny Saturday morning, I kissed our kids goodbye and drove myself to a therapist, clinging to the belief that everything was going to be all right. *This person is going to help me save my marriage*, I thought as my heart began to flutter, *I just know it!*

The therapist was a balding man in his fifties. He patiently listened to my story and then, pushing his glasses up his nose, announced with authority, "Well, you can't teach an old dog new tricks."

What? I couldn't even believe what I was hearing.

Amazingly, it took going to three therapists to find someone who was in line with my beliefs. Travis Smith's office was not the most impressive, but a familiar peace came over me when I stepped into that office; it was reassuring. How strange that I had never been there but felt so comfortable. My worries that he would be like the rest melted away as soon as I made eye contact with Travis. I could just feel that he was a humble, unassuming man. The moment I started to talk, he was 100 percent present with his mind and heart. When I finished, he smiled kindly. "I can support you in your decision to stay," he said. "We can do everything possible to help your marriage thrive."

Fighting for My Family, Marriage, and Community

For the next year I dove into my counseling sessions and assignments. Determined to be true to myself and save my marriage, I did every single thing Travis Smith encouraged me to do. Andy even came along to most of the sessions. I felt hope—as if we weren't shattered to pieces, but that we were gluing some major cracks together and were going to be better and stronger for having gone through the hard.

Serving and Earning and Saving Our Daughter: A Business Saved My Sanity and Our Daughter's Life

In Spring 2015, in the midst of all the emotional marital chaos, one of my daughters became extremely ill. The doctors tested her for everything. First, they thought she had cancer, then leukemia, and even kidney failure. When we got the diagnosis of celiac disease, you can only imagine the joy it was to learn that we weren't doing chemo or dialysis, but we were merely going *gluten free*. Of course, nobody wants to go gluten free, but that seemed way more appealing than the alternatives.

A lot of changes had to take place. Our kitchen had to have a complete overhaul, and I suddenly became aware of every little crumb in my home. All of my life's work of learning how to adapt to hard and challenging times played into my role of getting through yet one more trial thrown my way.

I quickly found my new passion to help others along our gluten-free journey. I started a blog and an Instagram account to document our journey and help others. Some people say I am crazy for all that I do. But little do they know, I did it mostly consciously and a little subconsciously *for survival*. I needed my brain and heart to survive, and the only way I knew how to do that was to stay busy and serve others.

I have always worked hard—fourteen siblings, I had to be self-sufficient and hustle my way through life. Making money was something I first learned when I was in 3rd grade and we didn't have money for school lunches. The first time, I pulled out my bag of three homemade chocolate-chip cookies; I decided to sell them for $1.25 to cover the cost of a hot lunch meal. That first time was the scariest. I was surprised when I didn't have just one taker, but five kids asked if they could buy my cookies each day for the next week. I was in business.

2016–2019: Wandering through My Marriage

There I was, fighting and wandering through my marriage, navigating through this new gluten-free life. I clung to every ounce of hope I could muster. I was determined that I was going to come out triumphant—that my family would be made whole. We would be an incredible statistic that made it through the trenches and back!

After all, every time I prayed, read my scriptures, meditated, or wrote in my journal, I received an overwhelming and very real prompting that I should stay in my marriage. So that's what I did. I stayed. I didn't stay because I was weak, scared of the what-ifs, or worried about what others would say. I stayed because I knew I wasn't done fighting for my marriage.

This was such a personal and specific answer from God to me. I couldn't deny it. So, I was on the road alone. Let's face it—since we can't physically see God or feel Him ALL the time, and since my counselor wasn't with me twenty-four/seven, I was pretty much alone most of the time. I was carrying my own cross.

Learning to Choose Joy

One night, long after the kids were in bed, I curled up on the couch with a cup of hot chocolate and wrote a question in my journal: *Why is God asking me to stay in this hard marriage? Does He want me to be unhappy and bitter?* I knew the answer to this question was no, and I decided that if I was choosing to stay in my marriage, I was going to choose to find the joy in my marriage. The blessings in the storm.

If I was going to change my focus, I knew I needed even more help than the counselor had given me. At that point, something President Russell M. Nelson said popped into my mind: "The joy we have has little to do with the circumstances of our lives, and everything to do with the focus of our lives."

I knew the principle President Nelson taught was true, but not knowing how to implement it was frustrating and discouraging. Nevertheless, I held onto hope. How could I find joy in this storm? Would Andy be willing to change to save our marriage? I had seen the counselor for a year, until I felt like he done everything he could to help me. It was now 2019, and for the last two years I had been on this journey without his help.

One night, lying in bed, I turned to Andy and said, "I'm really having a hard time feeling connected to you. I feel like we are two ships crossing in the night. We aren't in sync right now, and I am worried we are drifting apart in a scary way."

Andy looked at me and said, "I'm sorry; life is just busy."

I looked back at him with hope. I wanted to know that he was on the same page, that I wouldn't have to find that elusive joy by myself. But before I could say another word, he turned over and his breaths deepened into contented snores.

I was alone and deflated. How much more could I give?

To my surprise and relief, there was someone who was willing to walk with me on my path of finding joy. Jamee is a life coach who had been referred to me by a friend. Little did I know the impact she would have on my life.

I had no idea 2019 and 2020 would be the last years of our marriage, but during that time, Jamee helped me to work on my thoughts. As it turned out, that was a particularly great blessing, because Covid-19 also hit us hard—and I needed all the extra help I could get to survive mentally under quarantine and suddenly becoming a teacher to a kindergartener, first-grader, third-grader, and fourth-grader.

Jamee taught me to be keenly aware of what I allowed my mind to focus on and believe. Becoming intentional about my thought process was more work than I ever imagined, but the payoff was the very hope and joy I had been seeking amidst the hard.

The Nightmare Coming True

Two days after our twelve-year anniversary I found Andy lying on our bed with a helpless and hollow expression on his face. Sitting next to him, I looked into his brown eyes and knew from a place deep in my gut that he had nothing more to give. He was done fighting for us.

"Andy, you need to tell me what is going on." I pushed the words out despite my turning stomach and the pressure building in my head.

He swallowed hard and locked his gaze out the window. "I just can't tell you, Coral. I've hurt you so much already. I can't hurt you even more."

I let my body collapse beside him. "It's over then. Isn't it?"

After the years of fighting for our marriage, this is how it ended. No yelling or arguing, just a somber numbness. Everything in the room felt thick, as if we were in a hazy cloud. Divorce ruined my family when I was a child, and here I was reliving it.

"Can I call the kids up from downstairs to tell them I am leaving?" Andy asked.

That made it official. He was for real. It was over. Our marriage had failed.

Andy sat across from us with his back against the wall as Sadie fell in my lap and the other three children surrounded me.

"I have made some bad choices," Andy said, his eyes filling with tears, "and I need to leave. You guys are staying with Mommy."

Andy cleared his throat and looked at them straight in the eyes. "I want you to know that this is my own fault," he said. I could feel his deep sincerity and desperation to help them understand. "None of you did anything wrong."

Sadie began to shake in my lap, and Aliyah and Gavin broke into sobs. Chanelle tried to break the tension by making silly jokes.

We sat on the floor and cried for what seemed like hours. Time stopped. *Was this really happening?* He said goodbye to the kids and packed up his things and left. *How could this be real life?*

After Twelve Years, He Was Gone...

"Jamee, he left for good." With the kids tucked in bed, I locked myself in my closet and I slid down the back of the door, suddenly five hundred pounds. "All my fears are coming true," I sobbed.

She listened to me cry and then said softly, "Coral, divorce isn't the bad thing—what led to the divorce is what was bad."

The truth of those words struck me to the core. What if, in this case, the divorce *wasn't* bad? What if what *led to the divorce* was bad? My heart lightened the tiniest bit. I felt confident I had nothing to do with what led to the divorce. I knew that I had no regrets and had fought my best fight for our marriage. And I knew God had seen my every effort. Holding on to this belief in my heart felt peaceful and empowering. It was time to move forward.

A New Beginning

What do I do now? Seemed to run through my mind like a spinning hamster wheel. I didn't like this new reality at all. But all of my counseling and coaching prepared me to tackle this scary moment.

I had a crazy idea to move to Utah, where I had friends, family, and business connections. Over the next few days, I sat in front of my computer and pleaded with the Lord.

"Lord, If I am supposed to move to Utah, please show me a home that I can be excited about." I opened my laptop and there it was. A beautiful home in a nice neighborhood that was within my budget. I could see myself living there and loving it. It was 612 miles away and seemed so far … but I knew that the Lord was paving the way to my new start.

June 6th

One week after Andy left, I had packed up our entire life and driven my four children to Utah to start a new adventure!

I sat behind the wheel of the U-Haul and bid California goodbye in the rearview mirror. I had survived seven years of internal turmoil, and now I was free. I realized, though, that I didn't just survive; I found joy along the way. The fact that I had been able to choose happiness in the midst of so much strife was a miracle to me.

Tears fell from my face, but they weren't all from sadness. They were from a mixture of moving on, hope for a new life, and a sudden excitement that I was now in control of creating the rest of my story. Chanelle and Sadie giggled as they played in the back seat, and I glanced back at the sun shining softly through the window on their innocent faces. I felt its warm rays fall on me as well, and my shoulders relaxed at the thought that they too had a new opportunity for a good and happy life.

Chapter 2

EVERY SINGLE EMOTION

"Jamee, I think this is it; I think I am done in my marriage. Nothing even crazy dramatic happened recently; I just feel done. I'm tired of trying so hard. Every. Single. Day. I'm emotionally drained. I want out."

I will never forget the day I sent that text to Coach Jamee. My emotions ran so high, I almost gave up. I will also never forget the actions I took to make a better choice.

In this chapter we'll discuss how to stay in peace when emotions run amok.

We will learn what to do when emotions are so strong you can barely see straight.

It's vital to let yourself feel emotions, and it's also vital that you not let them run the show. When was the last time you made a great decision while riding high on emotion? When you make big decisions in your life—like the decision whether to stay or leave—you want to come to the table with peace and power and thoughtfulness. You absolutely do not want to be overwhelmed with anger, sadness, or discouragement.

In this chapter you'll learn how to respect and process feelings. You'll discover how your thoughts create your emotions. I'll share my discovery that if I wanted to experience healthy emotions, I needed to change my thoughts.

I'll also share with you personal examples of some hard emotions I have experienced. This isn't the surface stuff. This is the real deal. The hard. The ugly. The necessary. And the hope! You'll learn how *thoughtful* mind shifts can change your life for more joy.

The Game Plan

On the day I sent Jamee the text about being ready to leave, when my cup was empty and I just wanted out, I decided to pray again—more of a plea, really. I was surprised at the answer I got.

This time, I went to my favorite place of worship—a religious temple—to pray. I felt a huge peace come over me, telling me I should stay. It wasn't a "stay forever" necessarily; it was just "right now, in this moment, STAY." I felt peace, I felt hope, I felt loved, and I felt heard. I have learned that when my emotions are running high, I need to stop—to pause. Then I need to rely on a higher power to help me. I don't always get an answer so immediately, but this time, I did. I felt inspired and created a game plan of how I was to refocus my mind.

I found the peace I was searching for. I felt there were certain things I needed to do to *stay* positive and to *stay* happy. For example, I felt a deep impression that I should not talk about how much my husband worked and was gone outside of the home. I needed to change my thoughts and realize that him working hard wasn't a problem. I needed to believe that.

After I got direction from God, I made a conscious decision to choose thoughts supporting that direction. When I chose those thoughts, emotions followed. It is amazing how my new thoughts had a direct correlation to more positive emotions. This meant I wasn't letting emotions be in charge. I was letting God steer my life. I was so much happier and had great hope for my marriage. I knew I was doing all that I could to choose joy in the present moment.

Here are the new thoughts I created to be able to stay — and not just stay but stay happily.

I made a firm decision that every time I thought *ugh, he's at work again*, I would focus instead on what a hard worker he was and how he supported our family. And the miracle of it all was that I truly felt happier with those thoughts. Those thoughts shifted my emotions, and I was in awe at the peace I found.

To this day, I'm still amazed by the power of this truth: Thoughts create emotions, which then create actions.

Here's what in this instance, my husband hadn't changed a thing. He still worked hard, long hours and still came home exhausted, the very circumstance that triggered being so upset prior to my spiritual experience. But I was able to change my thoughts. My response. I showed up differently. I showed up as my better self. And because of these small thought shifts, my actions changed. I love the fact that I can live — even in the hard moments — with no regrets.

Living with no regrets is the most freeing feeling. You can know that even though there are trials, you have done all that you can do to help yourself be happy, show up as your best mom-self, and be as the best wife you know how to be. That's true freedom. That doesn't mean you hide the hurt — you simply find ways to deal with it in a person way then choose to focus on hope.

Friend, I want you to be able to live with no regrets, *no matter what.* I know you can receive guidance from a higher power and let that guidance direct your life. I know you can choose thoughts that allow you to show up as your best self. Now is the time to ask yourself, What type of thoughts do I have? Are they fueling or draining me?

Feel Your Feelings

Some people might say that I'm trying to repress my feelings. That I shove them down. That I'm not processing my emotions in a healthy way. Here's how I answer that: we all have to experience "the hard" in our own way and in our own time. We can respect our feelings and let these feelings teach us what we need to learn while not letting them control the outcome.

So how do you do this? How can you feel the emotions in a way that helps and heals? How do you not dwell in them?

I learned the answer to these questions when Andy and I had been separated for three weeks. I had just moved to Utah to get a fresh start, and Andy had just come to visit the kids for the weekend. I let my thoughts get the best of me. I texted Coach Jamee with tears flowing down my cheeks and my heart literally throbbing with pain. This is our exact conversation. I copied and pasted it so you can see that this is real life.

> *Me: I'm in a moment …*
> *It was a fine weekend with Andy. He ended up staying here at the house.*
> *He left this morning … but I have this deep feeling that he is with someone now, like in*

a relationship ... I am trying to get my head right. But I just feel sick to my
stomach. It is all my assumptions ... but I think my hunch is right. 📱😥
If Andy really is in a relationship with someone else, I feel so betrayed. I feel furious. I feel sad. I feel replaced.

Jamee:
Put your hand on your heart. Always start with self-compassion.
Of course you would feel betrayed and furious and sad. And replaced. Anyone in this situation would. Others have been in this situation and they have felt this way too. This is totally normal to feel this way in this scenario.
What does that feel like in your body?
Explain those sensations in your body as if you were explaining to an alien who has never felt an emotion.
How would you talk to a friend if she was experiencing these emotions?
"This is so hard." or "I'm so sorry."
Talk to yourself this way. Don't allow any criticism of yourself.

Me:
Thank you. I will continue to do this exercise. 😔 😞

Having compassion for myself was the answer. I sat in this emotion like I was sitting with a friend, having empathy and sympathy. I became my own listening ear. I cried, I was sad, I was scared—and all of that was somehow really okay.

As I was texting Jamee, I wasn't ready to get over it. I wasn't ready to have an answer. And she knew that. Right then, in that moment of brokenness, my solution was compassion. It was a relief to know I didn't have to be ready right then for the next step, even though I'm naturally a fixer.

Acceptance

Here was her next reply:

Jamee:
And when you're ready, you can accept the situation. It doesn't mean that the situation is okay. It's just a way to stop all of the stories and drama in your mind.
Acceptance is conscious awareness. It is not denial. So, we're not pretending like everything's okay when it's not okay. That is not what acceptance is. It's saying, "This is what's happening. I acknowledge it in the present moment." The way you do this is to change the sentence: "If Andy is in a relationship with someone else, Andy is in a relationship with someone else."
Can you accept that it's happening and then look to what would help you feel better?

Me:
I am trying to find something that would help me feel better😊

Jamee:
You're not ready to move on if you can't think of anything. You gotta digest those emotions

After doing Jamee's self-compassion exercises, I was surprised to find acceptance was attainable. I knew it would take me a while to reach acceptance but seeing that it was attainable was the light at the end of the tunnel. Regardless of whether Andy was with someone else, I learned to accept it. Because one day I am sure it really will happen and now I have the tools to help myself accept that situation.

That night, the pain was still there; it just wasn't as intense. I was still sad—but it was manageable. I still needed some help from a few melatonin gummies to rest my mind deep enough to fall asleep. But I did. And I woke up feeling much better.

And do you know what is interesting? Nothing about the situation changed except my outlook. My thoughts changed as I learned to accept my worst fear: that my best friend could be with someone else. After practicing compassion and acceptance, my emotions were better intact. My acceptance was that this was crummy and that I can do hard things. I could make it another day. It was another opportunity for me to show up for myself and be better!

Friend, can you see how powerful your mind truly is? No matter what you are going through, no matter what you are facing, you have control over your thoughts.

Letting Go of Other People's Emotions

Not only did I have a lot to learn about the power of my thoughts and emotions, I also had some hard lessons to learn about other people's thoughts and emotions. Can you believe I truly thought I could control other people's thoughts and feelings?

I learned about letting go of others' thoughts and emotions when I was choosing to stay in my marriage. I realize so clearly now that I wanted Andy to have the same experiences, emotions, and blessings of getting closer to the Lord as I was. I wanted him to refine his life the same way I was refining mine.

But that's not the way it works.

His journey is going to look different from mine. I can't choose for him. I can't choose his thoughts for him and can't create emotions for him. He gets to put in his own work on his own time. Whatever that looks like for him, his journey is no reflection on me whatsoever. Man, that was a hard reality.

I can remember this even for my children. I can let my children feel their emotions instead of me personally taking responsibility for their happiness. For example, my son came to me and cried; he was sad and scared about this new life we were creating without his dad. I held him and we cried together. I wanted to sugar-coat things, tell him how great it was going to be, and come up with all the things I could to entice him to brush off those hard emotions. But I didn't. I let him sit in those hard emotions. And I held him in the process.

Messy Emotions Are Okay

Are you ready for some irony? As I am writing this chapter, I am feeling angry. Emotions really are all over the place! Last night, I couldn't sleep. I feel angry as I wonder, *Why did Andy do this to me? I chose him. Why didn't he choose me forever like we promised? Why do I deserve to have to go back to the drawing board to find a new Mr. Right? I wanted it to be him so badly.*

So, today I feel mad. And that's okay. I am embracing the mad that I have to be alone right now and the mad that I have to figure life out and make decisions all by myself. Mad that I have to look for someone new who is honest and will be loyal and faithful and a good father. I am feeling all of the feelings. Today I am hanging out with anger. **My best friend betrayed me.** That is hard. Of course I am feeling sadness and anger. I mean, what human wouldn't have those feelings?

I am so glad that I am human. And I am even more grateful that I have the tools to work through these emotions. I can accept this "hard," and I can love myself while feeling all of these emotions.

Nine days after Andy left us, I packed up my entire life into one moving truck. I was so strong. I did it in a week. Seriously, anyone who has moved after having four kids in one home knows what a challenge this is. I did it like a boss. But, man, did I have a lot of emotions. I walked around crying all the time. I heard Chanelle say, "Sadie, don't say that. That's going to make mom cry." I heard Gavin say to Aliyah, "Don't show mom that picture—she'll cry." They were trying to protect me. But the funny thing is, I didn't mind crying. It wasn't a problem. Of course I cried.

I am supposed to feel everything I have felt and am still feeling, I am supposed to feel it on my own timeline. I can sit in each emotion for as long as I want or need. I can have compassion for myself. And then, when I am ready to move on and feel something different, I can. I can choose **happy** whenever I am ready!

I know that you are sitting in some pretty hard emotions right now too. Friend, you have been through so much. Of course you have all of these feelings. When you are ready, I want you to pause and focus on your thoughts.

Are they serving you? What emotions are they creating? Can you see the light or hope ahead? I am begging you to take a moment for yourself, have some compassion, as Jamee had me do; talk to yourself as if you are talking to a friend. What would you tell that friend? And when you are ready to find the next hopeful thing, when you are ready to change your thoughts, then you can change your emotions, which will then allow you to show up as your best self **no matter what!**

Deep Conversations with Coach Jamee

A study done at Stanford University discovered that our emotions—the chemicals and hormones that are released from our brains and into our bodies—have a lifespan of about ninety seconds. You often think that a negative or uncomfortable emotion will last *forever*, but the truth is that the chemicals will be digested and felt for about ninety seconds.

You can handle any emotions and not die. Even though your brain thinks anything uncomfortable—including your own emotion—is a threat and that you can't handle it, the more you practice just allowing the emotions to digest, the more evidence you will gather that you can handle anything! This is a key to gaining more and more confidence!

As you practice digesting your emotions, you will notice that the emotions feel like the waves of the sea, just coming and going. Your body knows what to do with these chemicals, just like it knows how to digest the lunch you ate today. You can just feel and allow the chemicals and not have to worry about doing anything about them.

Something you can practice is not identifying with your emotions:

You are not sad; you are FEELING sad.

"I am" statements are very powerful and sometimes are not helpful when navigating your way through life. Instead of saying "I am sad" or "I am depressed" or "I am annoyed," try saying something like "I am feeling sadness" or "I am experiencing the symptoms of depression." You are so much more than an emotion. Emotions are just sensations you experience in your body. You are separate from your body and emotions. Yes, your emotions belong with you, and you learn from them, but you are not an emotion.

Chapter 3

MORALS IN UNCHARTED TERRITORY

A week after I moved here to Utah—two weeks after Andy left our family—Andy came to visit the kids. He drove nine hours to get there. He was going to get a hotel, but I truly felt fine with him sleeping in the kids' room with them, and the kids were so excited.

But when I really stopped to think about it, that seemed like a crazy idea. I mean, we are in the thick of a divorce, and I am okay with him sleeping under the same roof? What was I doing? What was I thinking? What would others think of me allowing this? What was I supposed to do? How do I be true to my morals in this scenario?

In this chapter, I share what I chose to do and why I made that choice. After all, every single step I make now is uncharted territory.

I learned from a young age what types of choices bring what kinds of consequences—both the good kind and the bad. I have certain beliefs—standards or morals—because of what I have experienced. It doesn't always make me right or wrong; it makes me ME! I try to be good and make the right choices for me. I used to be bothered when people told me I was a "goody-goody." But I have learned to appreciate that as a compliment instead.

I choose my choices strategically because I want certain outcomes. But I have also learned through the years that different stages of life bring about different beliefs and morals. And that is what life is all about. I've learned to adapt, pivot, and continue to be true to who I am—and, more important, who I want to become. In this chapter I will open up and share with you how I learned how to find joy **no matter what** my situation or what others around me— including my own husband—believe their morals to be.

Identities and Report Cards

All my life I have had the goal of being one with my husband. In the Bible, we read that husbands and wives are to be one with each other. Being in a difficult marriage really had me question what that even meant.

Through the years, I have learned that I can strive to be one in my marriage, but what trumps that is the need to be one with God. He is my constant. I did strive to be one in my marriage. However, there came a time when it was healthy and helpful to let go of the belief that my husband and I would always be "one." Once I realized that my husband's thoughts and actions did not have to be the same as my thoughts and actions, I let a lot of frustration, sadness, and hopeless feelings go.

I have worked hard to put my identity as a child of God above any other identity, including that of a wife. I used to feel that how my spouse acted defined who I was as a person. It felt like how he acted reflected 100 percent on me, as if he was my report card! But I have learned that how my spouse acts does not define me as a person at all.

Ultimately, your spouse is not your report card. It's the same as your child doing something bad — that doesn't mean you were a bad parent and you get a *D* or an *F*. I think we all know of a few instances where amazing parents have unruly children and sometimes unruly parents have the best children. The same principle is true with a spouse. Their actions are not your actions. Their morals are not always the same as your morals. You get to decide if that is okay. But ultimately, your spouse is not your report card!

For years, I don't think I quite believed this principle. Maybe you can relate to the following experience — which, by the way, feels silly as I look back on it. We were out to dinner with a group of friends, laughing and having a great time. My husband cracked a joke that to me wasn't funny; in fact, it was insulting. So, I kicked him under the table and just prayed he didn't say anything else that was rude or embarrassing. I mean, I wanted our friends to continue to want to hang out with us and not be offended by something he said. I had good intentions with my silent and discreet "love kick." I felt I was doing the right thing. After all, I would want to know if I said something rude.

Without realizing it, I was thinking *his* words and actions defined *my* character and values. I was horrified to think these people would wonder if I too would put people down. While it is true that who I marry can reflect on me, it is not true that his words and actions define me as an individual. Instead of trying to get him to show up as a reflection of me, I can rest assured that he is his own person with his own identity. His trials and mistakes may affect me, but they are part of his individual journey. In fact, when I try to change and manipulate him in these stressful circumstances, I take away from his important life lessons to learn and grow.

What If My Spouse Has Different Morals than I Do?

The hardest part of our marriage was that my husband and I disagreed on the specifics of our morals. Actions that were tolerable for him but not tolerable for me rubbed on our marriage like sandpaper. To complicate the issue, I knew our situation was not ideal in the traditional sense of a "good Christian marriage." I was afraid to discuss my situation with friends, neighbors, and fellow church-goers. Would they judge me for staying when they hadn't walked in my shoes? I worried judgments would be made and my choices in our roller-coaster of a marriage would be a hard pill for others to swallow. After all, it was a hard pill for me to swallow. Every. Single. Day.

But here is the truth that finally set me free: my choices and morals are not other people's business. Events transpired that allowed me to dive deeper and clarify my own morals. This experience reminded me of parenting. Before I was a mom, I said, "I would never allow my child to act like that in public." But then I had kids, and I realized all kids come with different personalities. I realized too that I had been pretty naïve all those years earlier, because my child just threw the biggest fit in aisle three—and I fully gave in to what that child wanted.

Marriage is similar. How many times have you said, "I would never stay with someone who did [fill in the blank]." And then you experience that very thing and realize, *Wow, perhaps I can handle this. Or maybe I can forgive that particular behavior.* Some people allow their spouse to come home drunk or high in front of their kids, and they decide that is okay. Some people have open marriages. And that works for them. But that may not be what you want, so that wouldn't work for you. But you can then learn to be more neutral and less judgmental about others' choices and morals. You also need to give yourself grace. Until you are put in the circumstance, you truly do not know what you are willing to go through and endure.

For me, the real solution was to examine my morals and pick out what was most important to me. Even if my husband and I disagreed, it was okay for me to stay. And I found joy in that! Once I made my own clear decision about my morals and what I felt good about, I was able to have less anxiety about my husband's choices. I was able to focus on the positive. I love the words by Tony Robbins: "Energy flows where focus goes." As I understood and was true to my morals, positive energy flowed into our imperfect marriage.

I think it is safe to say we all want a fairy-tale love story. But the older I get and the more experiences I go through, the more I realize that I get to be the one to decide what that fairy tale looks like—even if that means I am not 100 percent deeply and madly in love with my spouse every single day. Maybe I create a fairy tale love story that goes something like this: Two people strive to stay in love as they navigate the hard in life. ... With opposition in all things and the very fact that Satan is real, they still choose each other at the end of the day ... or maybe the end of the week or the end of the year.

Surprise! Morals Can Change

I always fully believed it when I told myself I would never get a divorce.

Yet, here I am.

I'm in the thick of filing for a divorce I never wanted.

The craziest thing is that I have come to be 100 percent at peace with my choice. As I mentioned, when Andy first left, Coach Jamee said, "Coral, divorce isn't the bad part. What led to the divorce is what is bad."

After truly believing for my whole life that divorce was the worst thing ever, I let that lie go. I let go of the belief that divorce was the end of my life—like suddenly hitting a wall. I was simply opening a new door that had been pounded on for years. I had been afraid that by getting divorced, I was letting go of my morals. I now have a deeper understanding of my morals. My deepest moral is to be true to God, myself, and my children. Sometimes, that means getting divorced.

In my church—The Church of Jesus Christ of Latter-day Saints—we have the opportunity, if we choose and if we are worthy, to be married and sealed for time and all eternity in the holy temple. There we make covenants and promises that assure us that our family relationships will continue after this life if we remain true to our promises. And if we do, nothing, not even death, can separate us.

I did that. I made deep promises/covenants with God that I would remain faithful to my marriage. So, what does this divorce mean for me? Am I breaking my promises? Absolutely not! I know the Lord knows that I gave my marriage everything I had. I also know the Lord would not want me to suffer any longer. I know this because I have established my relationship with God as my foundation from the very beginning. I have turned to Him through all of the hard years. He is the one who gave me strength to stay and He is the one who is now giving me the strength to leave.

Some people look or even say things to imply I am doing something morally wrong to my children by leaving. People have also told me that divorce is going to hurt my children. Of course, my children are going to hurt. I of all people know divorce hurts children; I lived through my own parents' divorce. I also know I want to show my children that my highest moral value is self-worth and that I have self-worth. Ultimately, I want to show them by example that they are a child of a loving Father in Heaven and are truly royalty. Sometimes being royal comes with a heavy responsibility of standing up for yourself and your morals!

I know so many people who have chosen to stay in a bad marriage for their children. It was their moral value to not break up their family. But what I have found so interesting is that many of those who stay in a suffering relationship—I am not talking about surface disagreements; I am talking about very deep-rooted abuse or addictions or other matters that have serious consequences—have children who most often go on to continue the cycle of dysfunctionality and unhealthy relationships because that is what was modeled for them. You can ask yourself, *Is saving my children from the hurt of a divorce more important than breaking the cycle?*

Freedom Is Letting Go of Others' Morals and Judgments

Another struggle I have is when people I love, both family and friends, share their morals and expectations and feel that I need to have those same morals. I find it interesting that if others were to truly see the last years of my marriage, I would get judged on every side. Many would say, "Why would Coral stay in this marriage? Doesn't she know she is so much better than that?" Others may say, "Coral did the right thing by staying, because you should never leave a marriage."

I was finally set free from the prison of others' values and judgments when I came to understand that marriage and divorce are completely my choice. I do not need others' approval or disapproval. The best thing someone can do for me is to support me in whatever decision I choose. They aren't the ones who are living in the marriage, so why would they have a say as to what I do?

Something I have found interesting in the past few months is how friends, family, and even my new dentist have handled the fact that I am getting a divorce. Each person I have told has responded differently. There is a mourning process for them, and I need to remember that I have to give them time to process it as well. You may think, as I did at first, *It's not their business to have an opinion or emotions about my life.* But then I realized that I can be more understanding. This is the first time a majority of these people have heard that I had even struggled in my marriage. Of course, they care about me. Of course, they want to mourn with me. But there is a fine line; it is not my job to help someone process my life. Their thoughts are none of my business.

As harsh as that sounds, I need to work on myself and block out others' thoughts or ideas. It is healthiest for me to remove distractions and extra noise. To be honest, I don't like to be around when someone first hears the news of my divorce because their moral response truly isn't my business.

It is kind of like when you are about to have a baby and you are picking a name for that child: everyone has a strong opinion on names. Like their opinion matters—*no way*! But for some reason, people—and generally those we love the most—can be the most critical and opinionated. Ultimately, it is none of their business.

Marriage is also none of anyone else's business. If you are being abused in any way, I hope that those you love to step in and provide the support and help you need. But other than that, whether you stay in a hard marriage or leave a marriage is 100 percent up to you and the Lord.

I find it rather sad now that I have the title of *divorced*; it's like a free pass for others to openly judge my ex-husband. That is exactly what I don't need right now. Is he an idiot for letting us all go? Of course. I know that; he knows that. It isn't what any of us want. But it is what certain choices have led to. He is still the father of my children. I want them to grow up knowing their dad loves them more than anything. When other people jump to a conclusion and say how stupid he is, they have no idea how hard it is for both him and me. We have gone through so much. So, when someone says horrible things about him, I find myself getting defensive for him.

Through months of processing, I have learned that I don't need to defend him or play into any more drama with the situation. So now, when someone says something bad about Andy, I choose to say something along the lines of, "Yes, isn't life hard? And it's so wild how each of us has trials to overcome, some bigger than others." This isn't a dramatic play. This is my life. This is my kids' life. And we are trying to create our best life without playing into any more drama! I am choosing to be more neutral about the situation as a whole, and ultimately, I am so appreciative of others when they support my moral decisions.

I have incredible neighbors on my street, and I am forever grateful for their warm welcome and the help they gave while I was moving in! There are so many amazing, good, Christian families right on my block. When Andy was coming up to visit us two weeks after filing for divorce, I was so torn on how I was supposed to show up, what my morals were, and what my morals were looking like to others.

At first, I thought that it would be strange, almost wrong, for the neighbors to see Andy's truck in the driveway all night. What would they think? I mean, they just sent all their husbands over to unload my massive U-Haul the week before because I was a single mom. And then Andy comes the next week and is spending the night?

But I stopped those thoughts. I made a conscious decision to shift away from the worry of others' thoughts and morals. I knew getting caught up in these toxic thoughts would create toxic feelings. If I have catty or gossipy neighbors, let them be. If others want to talk about me, I am totally okay with that. They have no idea what I am going through. These new thoughts fueled me and gave me the courage to do exactly what I felt morally good about in that moment. Later, it was so refreshing to learn that my neighbors didn't share their opinions at all, and I felt so much love from them. They didn't know what I was going through, and no one seemed to bat an eye at my decision. So why would I let those self-created thoughts factor into my decision at all?

I know that I am doing the best I can with what I have been given. I have that strength, I have that confidence, so **no matter what** others may say or do, I know that I am doing my personal best with the morals I have! And by the way, I really do have the best neighbors ever!

Deep Conversations with Coach Jamee

Worrying about what others think is just a part of being human. We are all going to worry about what others think, because we want to feel connected to others and we want to feel supported in our decisions. It is a basic human desire and need to feel connected and supported. So, when you notice that you are worrying about what others think, first and foremost, be kind to yourself. You want to feel connected to others and supported, and it is okay to want this.

One of the problems with making decisions off of what someone else might think of you is that you really have no idea what others will think of you. There are hundreds of thoughts they could be thinking at any given moment, and you have no way of knowing exactly which one they may be choosing to believe.

Another problem with trying to please people is that someone else has no idea what is best for you. They don't have all the information. Even if you were able to share with them every detail of your life, they would still be missing your own feelings and your own experience. And they have no idea what you are supposed to be learning right now through this experience!

A third problem with trying to please people is assuming you or anyone else shouldn't be going through a certain experience. How do you know if someone is having an experience he or she isn't supposed to have? How does someone else really know what you should do? How do you know what the learning is, and how does someone else know what you should or should not be learning?

God is more concerned with your growth and learning than He is with your struggling. We always learn through our struggles. You may notice that others are struggling, and you may want the struggle to be taken away. But how do you know if that isn't the exact struggle someone needs right now to learn exactly what God wants them to learn?

This is the truth: you are the best one to make decisions for your life. One solution to trying to please people is to choose to believe that whatever you decide to do is a good decision. Your decisions are good, because you have the power to learn from each decision and to make that decision good. Others will always have their thoughts and opinions, and they may choose to disagree with what you are doing, but they are also allowed to be wrong about you. Can you allow others to be wrong about you and also make decisions in your life based on what YOU think about YOU and not what others may think? You can say to yourself, "They may think such-and-such about me, and that's okay, because they don't know the best thing for me to do anyway."

It's no one else's job to approve of you. That's your job!

Chapter 4

BOUNDARIES ARE A BLESSING

Boundaries seem to have such a negative rep. I'm just as guilty as the next person—when I hear someone say, "I need to set boundaries with so-and-so," I think, *Oh yikes, there is a problem.* My mind immediately thinks of a boundary as an ultimatum or something negative—a line that someone else can't cross. I remember sharing a desk in elementary school and making an imaginary line that my desk mate was not allowed to cross.

What if we flip that around? Instead, what if I think of it as the line that *I* will not cross? I've learned that these lines I draw for myself can protect me. A boundary can be my blessing!

Jamee's definition of a boundary allowed me to accept and be grateful for boundaries. She taught me that a boundary is a line that you draw to support and control *yourself*—not the other person. A boundary isn't telling someone else what he or she can't do. A boundary is knowing when *you* will say "no." A boundary lets you love yourself and others more.

A boundary is stated as, "If you do this, then I will do this." An example of a boundary is, "If you yell at me, then

I will leave the room," or, "If you yell at me, then I will hang up the phone." You're not controlling someone by telling him to stop yelling; you're telling him what you will do if he continues his behavior. He can choose to continue his behavior, and because you've set a boundary, he clearly knows what *you* will do if he continues.

You can set boundaries out of love for the other person — because when there is no boundary set, you might feel resentful and frustrated toward the other person. Instead of "attacking" the other person, you are taking care of yourself. Boundaries protect your values and your time.

If there is a lesson I have learned, it is that I cannot control anyone but myself. So, I stayed true to who I was. Regardless of what is happening around me, I have values and standards to which I will stay true.

My Boundaries

I struggled to know what my boundaries were while I stayed in my hard marriage. But just this morning I had an "aha" moment. Without even realizing it, I became aware that I have always had boundaries! I had them for years in my marriage and didn't even recognize it. My boundaries were the things on which I was not willing to compromise. For example, I was never going to compromise my safety and my children's safety and well-being. I was not going to compromise the desire to feel the Spirit in my home. My boundaries are set to take care of and protect me.

One boundary I created without even realizing it was to make enough time for myself and the Lord every day. I didn't recognize it as a boundary, but it was. I literally had to read scriptures, pray, and surround myself with good things for my own survival. It was such a refining process for me to learn who I am and my own self-worth, independent of anyone else. Without this boundary, I wouldn't be where I am or who I am today. I had to stay within my personal sphere or boundary that was safe and comforting in the hardest of times. That is how I survived.

Every day was not perfect. There were countless days I missed my scripture study. But guess what? When I stepped out of my boundary or "safety zone," things were hard, and I felt uncomfortable. I didn't like how I felt those days. I didn't like the negative thoughts I had, and I didn't like who I showed up as. So, I would hurry back into the boundaries I set for my own personal and spiritual success. That is how I survived and thrived and found the joy! I want to note that Andy was and is not a horrible person; he has always supported me and respected my boundaries. Because of the respect he had for me, I could stay as long as I did. This may not be the case in every scenario, but that's how my personal journey looked.

Boundaries have played an important role in my process of accepting my trials. For so many years, I tried to pray problems away, saying things like, "Please, Lord, I'm at my wits' end." Recently I decided that I want to pray a little differently. My boundary around prayer is that instead of trying to pray my problems away, I pray to have the strength and tools to get me through the trial. I pray to learn what I'm supposed to learn from a trial instead of wishing it would just go away.

It's important for all of us to go through certain trials. Think of the Savior Himself, when in the Garden of Gethsemane He asked, "Father, if thou be willing, remove this cup from me ..." (Luke 22:42). The Savior had to experience the ultimate pain of sin and sickness and emotion, pain that caused Him to bleed from every pore; He continued, "nevertheless not my will, but thine, be done." If I am trying to be more like Him, I guess I need to go through my own Gethsemane at times. The boundaries that I set and commit to are what help me get through these times with Him by my side.

Friend, let's get deep. What are you doing to protect yourself and your boundaries? What holds the most value in your life, and what boundaries will protect it? What are you not willing to compromise? Setting boundaries may feel a bit dramatic at first. But I am here to offer you relief from those thoughts and feelings. Boundaries are not dramatic and do not have to feel extreme. It is actually quite the opposite. Boundaries offer you the freedom to live guilt free. When a boundary is set with intention and from a place of love, you may be providing others with exactly what they need to learn and grow. Without those boundaries, you may be enabling a hurtful process.

Others' Boundaries

As you can imagine, I wanted to create Andy's boundaries. I wanted him to act and live a certain way. Have you ever tried to create a boundary for someone else? If you have, you know it doesn't work. Change has to stem from each person—it has to be his or her idea. If it's not, you may see a change for a day, a week, or even a year. There were several times in my marriage that I did see Andy's boundaries change. I had hope. I was filled with joy. But because those boundaries were for me and not for him, there was no long-term change.

One night jumps out at me so clearly. I was lying next to Andy in bed crying, trying to muffle my sobs so he wouldn't know the hurt his lack of boundaries had caused me. Why didn't he change? Didn't he want the good life we could have together? What could I do to help him change?

Laying there, I thought about what Jamee had taught me—that my thoughts created my feelings. My thoughts were that he didn't care enough to truly change. I sat with that thought. I wondered what emotion it was creating. It was creating the emotion of feeling like a victim. I knew I was not a victim. I am the hero of my own story. I truly believe that. I believe everyone is the hero of his or her own story. So, I asked myself "What would a hero do? What thoughts would they have?"

That night led me to so much inward contemplation— another "a-ha" moment. In fact, it may be one of the most refining moments of my life. Even though I was not at fault for the major struggles in our marriage, I searched inwardly for solutions. That is what heroes do. I finally realized that I needed to stop trying to change his boundaries and focus on my own.

Over the weeks and months and a lot of phone calls with Jamee, I practiced creating and keeping my own boundaries. And do you know what happened? The most amazing miracle happened. Because I was clear and confident in my own boundaries, I was blessed with an added measure of love, compassion, and forgiveness for myself and for Andy. My strength did not come from drawing a line that he couldn't cross. My real power came from the lines I knew that I would not cross.

Can Boundaries Change?

Let's face it: life happens, circumstances change, and boundaries can change as well. Sometimes you need to tighten up a boundary, and sometimes it is good to let your boundary parameter extend a bit. Doing that is not changing your morals or lowering your standards. You are adapting to your situation and that is okay. I used to worry I was lowering my standards when I changed my boundaries. But I was wrong.

As I mentioned earlier, the first time Andy came to Utah to visit the kids, I was a mess inside. I panicked at first because I didn't have boundaries established for this scenario. I really felt fine having him come to visit the kids. But how could I have invited him to stay in my home? The truth is that after I offered, I started to overthink the entire situation and wasn't sure what I was supposed to do.

I called a friend and shared my struggles and feelings. A few of her words in particular comforted me and remain with me, even to this day. "It is okay that you don't know exactly what to do," she told me, "This is all uncharted territory." It *was* uncharted territory. It was completely fine that I didn't know exactly what to do.

The first time he stayed at my house, I was okay with it. But for the next visits, it just made sense for him to get a hotel.

There isn't a rule book for life. Sometimes I really wish there was. But as long as I am being true to myself and protecting myself and my children, I am going to be just fine.

As you navigate life and your circumstances change, it is normal and often necessary to establish new boundaries, without feeling any guilt or shame to go along with it. This is life. And I truly believe that we are all just trying to do the best we can with what we have been given!

Not too long ago, I had a good friend tell me that years ago she decided to stay in her tough marriage. She thought that because she made that decision, she had to stay forever. She was feeling weighed down and almost trapped. Once I announced that I was getting a divorce, she felt relief. My experience gave her the freedom that she could change her boundaries if needed. She realized she had the freedom to continue to choose what she wants and what boundaries she needs at each moment. She is in a really great place in her marriage right now. But just understanding that she always has a choice and in no way is trapped was freeing to her. She can always get out if she feels she needs to. Sometimes we need that reassurance or permission to do what is right in different moments.

I often get asked, "How did you make your marriage work for so long?" My new and favorite answer is, "I established boundaries." It was about my own personal boundaries, not his. Boundaries don't control the other person—they controlled and protected me, and I know they can protect you as well.

As you read through these chapters, I hope that you are contemplating the things that are true *to you*—the feelings *you* are having. Nothing I am saying that will change you so you will find more joy, but the very thoughts and impressions that you are having will change you! Remember, I can't change your boundaries either—that is all on you. But I am here to cheer you on and remind you that you can do this! You can do hard things!

Deep Conversations with Coach Jamee

Boundaries are the most important thing you can do to protect your intimacy and safety in your relationships. A lot of people think they have communication problems in their marriages, but the truth is that communication is not always the problem. A majority of the time the problem is that one or both feel unsafe. You may feel unsafe to be yourself, or there may be a level of distrust. Setting a boundary means that you are willing to continue in a healthy relationship with someone, because boundaries increase our love for yourself and for the other person.

Ironically, boundaries can be the most difficult part of a relationship to navigate. Why can boundaries be so hard? Sometimes people don't want to set a boundary because they don't want to feel frustrated or mean. But when you look at this closely, it's important to note that, without a boundary, you are probably already being mean. Without boundaries, you will often start feeling disconnected and resentful toward this person. Maybe you find yourself "fake smiling" as he is talking or you are looking for ways to avoid him. You may find yourself thinking an array of negative thoughts about him and talking about him in negative ways to others. When a boundary is set, you actually open the door to feel taken care of, and your soul will feel nourished. From that place you drop resentment and are able to keep a healthy relationship with someone as opposed to cutting him off forever.

Setting boundaries happens from a place of love for you and them. It's more like, "I love you and don't want to feel resentment toward you, so if this behavior continues then I will do [insert a non-controlling and nonthreatening action you will take]." You set that boundary instead of saying (or thinking), "I can't believe you did this, so now I hate you, and I'm never talking to you again!"

This goes in both directions. Let's say someone you have a relationship with sets a boundary; if you do not respect it, then you are not helping to create an environment of safety in the relationship. A simple example of this is if a friend asks you to please not stop by her house unexpectedly. You ignore that request, and when you stop by unexpectedly, you say, "It's not a big deal; you really need to get over your insecurities." A boundary doesn't need to make sense to you or the other person in order to be respected. When you respect boundaries then you create safety and healthy relationships.

With healthy boundaries in place, you get to feel anything that feels like love toward the other person **no matter what** the other person feels or says or does. That's what you're trying to create in healthy relationships. Regardless of whether you are staying married, a healthy relationship is truly what you want.

And never forget: sometimes love means saying, "No."

Chapter 5

WHAT ABOUT
THE KIDS?

W hen we moved to Utah, some of our furniture didn't fit in the new house, so I had to buy a few things. Our new recliner was my five-year-old daughter's favorite cuddle spot. She looked up at me with wide, hopeful eyes and asked, "Can we take this chair to California when we move back in two weeks?" I explained that we were not going back to California — that this would be our new home for at least a year. She looked at me with complete despair, ran away crying, hid under her bed, and would not come out as she sobbed, "I want Daddy."

Is a crystal ball too much to ask for? I mean, a girl can dream, right? If only I had a crystal ball to tell me what to do with my children. How much do I tell them about what is really going on? How do I let them feel their own emotions and still comfort and love them? Do I let them know how sad I'm feeling? The three parenting principles I will share in this chapter are what I wish someone had shared with me when I was in the thick of it all.

Three Parenting Principles

1. **Allow your children to FEEL,** even if that means they are sad for a time!

Just a few months after getting married, I heard in a marriage seminar we attended that if you fight in front of your kids, you should also kiss and make up in front of your kids. This principle has stuck with me all these years. This has allowed my children to know that there are trials, challenges, disagreements, and arguments, but that I also know how to apologize, to forgive, and to work through hard times and find the joy!

I remember one extremely hard day when the kids came home from school and my eyes were puffy and red as a tomato. There was no hiding or denying the fact that I had been bawling my eyes out for the past three hours. My heart hurt. My head hurt. It felt like I had a bad hangover. (I actually have never had a real hangover, but from what I hear, it felt I like the worst hangover ever.) Andy and I had just reached a sad turning point in our marriage.

When the kids walked in the door, they looked at me with so much worry and concern. One of them asked, "Mom, are you okay?"

"I am having a hard day," I answered. "I am feeling so sad. Do you ever feel sad?" I knew the answer, of course; they know how sadness feels. I was completely 100 percent fine with them knowing I feel sad sometimes too. Yes, I could have said my allergies were acting up. But what does that teach them? That when you are older you aren't allowed to have emotions? That you can't talk about your hard days?

I want my children to know that I have to learn how to deal with emotions too, even as a mom, just like they do.

At that time, I didn't feel a need to tell them the details of why I was sad. They just understood that life can be hard sometimes and that is just part of being human.

Then the sweetest thing happened: they were there for me. They tried to cheer me up, massaged my back, and brought me some of my favorite treats. And you know what? That helped me so much. At such young ages, they were able to help me—a thirty-four-year-old—feel a bit better. They took the sting off the pain. I truly believe that is what a family is for. We can be vulnerable and help one another all while showing real-life emotions. This experience would have looked a lot different had I tried to hide my emotions from my children and tried to pretend everything was okay!

Another more recent example of feeling emotions with my children was when we were sitting at the table, eating together and enjoying the fact that we had mastered a new gluten-free pizza crust recipe. Suddenly Sadie looked up at me and said, "Mom, when I see other kids with their dads, I get really sad."

My eyes filled with tears as I stopped to remember those exact feelings when I was young and wished I had a daddy to come home to! I looked at her and my voice broke as I said, "Oh, Sadie, I am sure that it is so hard to see others with their dads. Of course, that would make you sad. And you know something? I remember feeling that way when I was your age too! But your daddy loves you very much and you are going to see him very soon. You will have the best time with him." We held each other for a minute and the conversation moved on!

I was so grateful that she felt comfortable sharing her feelings. I'm so glad she can acknowledge the hard and even the sad. Because as we are creating a home where we share feelings together, we also get to share the moments of understanding and love.

2. Giving the kids a WHY

"But **why,** Mom?" How many times do I hear that a day?
Why do I need to brush my teeth?
Why do I need to make my bed?
Why do I have to eat my vegetables?

Sometimes the answer to a **why** is, "Because I said so." But other times, kids really need to understand the **why**. It is amazing that when I take the time to talk with my children and explain why we do certain things they actually respond so much better. Is it perfect? *No.* But it is helpful a lot of the time. And I can completely relate — if I know **why** I am doing a certain task, I am so much better at it!

When times are hard, I imagine what those cute little brains and hearts could be thinking and feeling. *Did my parents just fight because I wasn't being good? Am I the reason they are getting a divorce?* These are real struggles.

Let me share with you my personal experience when I was young. Looking back at my childhood with divorced parents, I appreciate that I understood the **why** of my parents' separation. My mom was very open with us kids. I was young when they divorced, but she was always open about the situation and was always there to answer my questions. I appreciated that. I understood that their splitting up had nothing to do with me and everything to do with certain actions that took place. Most would think that I would hold a lot of resentment and anger toward my dad after my mother shared what my father had done. But I realize now that it is what most helped me develop into the person I am today. I learned how to forgive and not judge at such a young age. It actually has helped me more than I have ever realized.

I can honestly say that I am grateful for having a hard childhood and for understanding the **why**. As I bounced from one parent to the other with fourteen siblings, it is safe to say that I did not have a "normal" family life growing up. How ironic that people in my life have often told me that I wouldn't understand a hard situation because my life is so blessed— that I have had everything "handed to me." That always blows my mind. Can they not see into my soul to know that I have fought for every achievement and success in my life? Maybe they do not see it because I learned many of my tough lessons at such a young age and I have learned to overcome, adapt, and find the joy. I knew my purpose, and I knew that I hadn't done anything wrong to have the family life I did.

My best advice for learning tough life lessons is to not wish or pray them away but to ask what we can learn from them—the earlier the better. If one had to choose between learning a lesson of forgiveness at age five or age fifty, I think most people would say they want to learn it at age five. Why? Because when you learn hard principles, like forgiveness, you are free from the burden or resentment you could have held onto for years.

I try to remember to allow my children to feel all of the feelings and not shield them from the tough stuff. Obviously, we protect our children from harm or danger. But they need to process feelings—and if you can be vulnerable with them, right alongside them, it will go so far.

I often hear a familiar concern from friends who are having a hard time in their marriage or even those who have chosen to divorce: They don't want to tell the kids the **why** because they don't want their kids to have to pick a side or be upset with the other parent. The problem with this is that if you don't give kids a **why,** they will come up with their own **why** in their head.

Let me be frank: Hearing the **why** is not always easy; it will take time to digest and process. But if you have the right tools and use with compassion and understanding the practices that Coach Jamee gives at the end of this chapter, kids can be the most forgiving and resilient of all humans.

I know every situation is different, and maybe your **why** can't be broken down detail by detail. But provide a **why** that is appropriate for the age of the child. For example, you might say to a younger child, "Dad has made some bad choices." If the child is older, you might talk about addictions, mental disorders, or whatever you are experiencing. Which leads right into the third topic I want to share with you...

3. What to share and how much to share

Knowing what and how much to share with kids can be so tricky, especially when it comes to kids of different ages and different personalities. Let's face it—kids don't come with a manual. Everything we do as parents is trial and error, but ultimately, we all hope for success.

For years, Andy and I had some serious problems in our marriage. Together we decided we were going to do our best to work through them. So, I gave it all I had. We went to counseling, went to therapy, took advantage of coaching, and read books together. Some days were really tough, and as I mentioned earlier, often it was obvious to my children that I was sad.

I eventually decided that it was okay for them to see me in my real emotions. If I knew they could have heard Andy and me talking or when I felt like it was appropriate, I opened up a bit more to them. I asked if they had any questions. I always allowed them to come to me and ask me anything. I was a safe place for them. That is very important to me as their mother. It was always a blessing when they opened up to me and asked me questions.

Because I was choosing to stay in my marriage, I felt it was important to keep details of our trials from my children. They didn't need to know specifics at that time. I knew then, as I still believe, that I will share more with them as they get older. But at that time, they knew that relationships can be hard.

I would not speak negatively about Andy. It is so important to not feed your emotions to someone else—especially your children. They understood that mom was sad with dad at times, but other than that, they were spared or protected from the details. That was very intentional. There was not a need for them to know any more than that.

Every time I think about the day Andy told me he needed to leave, I get tears in my eyes. After he told me he was leaving, he immediately asked if we should tell the kids. There wasn't a dry eye in the room. Watching each of my four children respond differently was so hard. I didn't want my kids to be sad. But they needed the **why**, and they needed to be sad. So, I let them. I didn't say a word. I just hugged them and cried with them at each opportunity.

It is now my opportunity to be real and raw with my children. We talk about making good choices in our lives. We talk about Satan and how real he is and how he will try to tempt us all. We talk about how we find peace and happiness in life. We talk about the Atonement and all that Jesus has done for us to ensure that we can be forgiven when we make bad choices. We talk about how Jesus knows how we feel when we are sad, hurt, or scared. We talk about how we can pray to Him when we are struggling. We talk openly and frequently about it all.

I can assure you that we all still get very emotional at times. But we are okay. Sadie, who wouldn't come out from under her bed because she only wanted her daddy, is doing so well as we focus on her FaceTime chats with him. She loves texting him the longest emoji texts with every facial expression character, ice cream, lollipop, and whatever else she feels he would love to see in that emoji moment.

The kids and I choose to love on each other when we are feeling down. We play together. We laugh together, and we cry together. All of these emotions are normal. They are necessary. Ultimately, I am so grateful that I can be open with my children, and together we are learning to deal with hard emotions.

It is draining, and it takes a lot of effort to work through tough emotions. But when you do, you can find the **joy** you so badly long for, for yourself and for your kids. I know you can do it. If I can do it, surely you can too! No matter what, whether you are staying or divorcing, you can help your children feel all the feelings and enjoy happiness when they are individually ready!

Deep Conversations with Coach Jamee

You are 100 percent responsible for your emotions and behaviors, and your children are 100 percent responsible for their emotions and their behaviors. This means that your children will suffer in some way, and they are allowed to feel whatever they want to feel. You are not responsible for taking away anything they are feeling. They are simply humans who are having thoughts, and their thoughts are making them feel an emotion.

We all love our children and don't like to see them suffer in any way, so we often feel like we need to fix their suffering and take away their negative emotions. We say things like, "Don't be sad," or we think of ways to take away their sadness.

However, when we do this, we are not helping our children as much as we think. Here is what is actually happening: If your child stops suffering, then *you* get to feel relief. As painful as it feels to allow our children to feel uncomfortable emotions, we must remember this is a part of the human experience. All humans experience hurt and a range of emotions. This is part of being alive!

When we try to take away their emotions, we actually add more stress and pressure to the situation. This doesn't mean that you aren't sad when your child is sad. You can be sad, and you can allow your child to be sad as well. In fact, showing your children you are sad helps takes the edge off of a lot of your uncomfortable emotions and helps model to your children how to do life in a healthy way.

Something else to remember is that the more we allow ourselves and our children to feel uncomfortable emotions, the more we open ourselves up to fully feel the emotions that feel good. Without the contrast of emotions, people start to feel neutral and numb to life. As a result, their capacity to feel happy decreases. Your brain has to be able to have opposition in order to notice the difference. If you allow sadness when sadness is there, then your brain will start to notice more delight.

One way to start seeing your emotions as okay and to welcome all of them in your life is to compare them to colors. We don't judge colors the same way we do emotions. We aren't walking around judging the color purple or saying things like, "White is so bad." We realize for both ourselves and our children that there is a time and place for every color. It's the same with our emotions. We can welcome them and learn from them instead of avoiding them or trying to fix them.

To help you in this area, try doing some journaling; following are some appropriate prompts you might want to use:

- What if your job as a mother (or father) is not to take away your child's experiences but to simply model for them how to embrace the whole human experience?
- What would it feel like to allow yourself and your children to feel anything they are feeling?
- How might you feel on a daily basis if you weren't responsible for your children's feelings and you weren't responsible for making them feel better?
- What might you say and do as a mother if you were modeling this for your children?

Chapter 6

CREATING YOUR OWN ROADMAP

I am strong and beautiful. I am a child of God. I have charity toward myself and others, and part of charity is having boundaries. I have hope that as I make the next right choice, I will be exactly where I am supposed to be!

Coral's Mantra

A mantra is typically a positive phrase or statement that you can use to affirm the way you want to live your life—a roadmap, if you will. My mantra is my personal affirmation that motivates and inspires me to be my best self. As I created specific goals about who I wanted to be and where I wanted to go, the road in front of me became crystal clear. As I experienced that clear focus, I no longer worried about the opinions of others. What a beautiful relief!

In this chapter, I am going to help you do the same. Through identifying your core values and creating your personal mantra, you will create a vision of where you are going. This is going to feel good!

Mantra Power

Years ago, when I first learned about my husband's problems and realized that I didn't have the ideal marriage I had always dreamed of, I was so distraught. I told myself that it was unacceptable. I knew I didn't deserve this. I knew that if others knew, they would tell me to run—but somehow, deep inside, I knew that I was going to be okay **no matter what**. Whether I stayed or left, I knew that my kids would be okay. Still, the internal struggle continued ...

How did I want to show up for myself?
How did I want to show up for my kids?
How did I want to show up for Andy?
How did I want to show up to the world?

I decided that I wanted to be true to the person I am and not allow others' actions or opinions to tear me down. I had to dig deep and evaluate my core values and who I was striving to be. Looking back through these trying years, there are three core values I have held tightly to and that have led me to be who I am today with literally zero regrets. It wasn't easy; actually, it has been so hard. I have had to intentionally check in with myself regularly and even reset when needed. I haven't been perfect, but I am always trying to progress and be a little better—and that is all I expect from myself! Not perfection, just progress!

This chapter is a little bit different from the other chapters in this book. Before I explain the values I chose, I want you to evaluate what core values are important to you. How do you show up as your best self? Knowing the answer is vital to creating your mantra. Your core values may include humility, trust, respect, love, dependability, reliability, loyalty, commitment, open-mindedness, strength, and honesty. Ultimately, what fuels you and helps you to live with no regrets and show up as your best self?

Before I talk about my values, I have an exercise to help you create a mantra for your life. You can recite it when you need to make a decision, you are having a hard time, or even when you need a good mental reset! Feel free to steal mine if that serves you, but I encourage you to do some soul searching and figure out what makes you thrive!

Create a vision of who you want to be. Like I said, this will look different for everyone. For example, the mantra for someone who is battling cancer may revolve around strength or fight, while the mantra who is struggling with forgiving others may revolve around humility and open-mindedness. Okay, I think you get the idea. Now it is your turn; here are a few questions and insights to help prompt you:

1. What do you want to feel right now, at this moment? For me, I know I want to feel perfect contentment, knowing I have exactly what I need. You might need to feel hope that circumstances will work out. You might need peace or acceptance of your current situation. Whatever it is, write it down.

2. Once you have figured out the feelings you want to achieve, turn those thoughts into a declarative statement; it will soon be tweaked into your personal declarative affirmation.

3. Write your statement in the first person; after all, this is for you! Use words like I am or I have or I will. This is the personal touch that will drive you to becoming the very person you long to be and to have the very feelings that you intentionally are striving to feel!

4. Avoid negative words, like not, never, and can't. Your goal is to be your most optimistic self. Keep your mantra positive so it can motivate and uplift you in hard times and with difficult decisions.

5. Write it. Recite it. Repeat it. The purpose of this is for you to respond and show up as the best you. This is not for anyone else's approval. This is for you to remember and recite when you need it the most. You can even write it on your mirror with lipstick so you see it and believe it when you wake up every morning!

I can't wait to hear what **your** mantra is and how it serves you! There is something so profound about deciding how you want to show up. My own mantra has served me in so many ways, especially within the past few months.

To review, my mantra is, "I am strong and beautiful. I am a child of God. I have charity towards myself and others and part of charity is having boundaries. I have hope that as I make the next right choice I will be exactly where I am supposed to be!"

Now that you have your mantra, you can move on to choosing core values.

Core Values

My core values are self-worth, charity, and hope.

Let me tell you what led me to these three core values and how they serve me. These three values don't always come easy for me. It takes a lot of mental work for me to feel peace and find true joy **no matter what** my circumstance is.

Self-Worth

I am not sure why I always had the most gorgeous girlfriends growing up; I had a lot of guy friends too because of it. I mean, if a guy was too intimidated to talk to my friend, he befriended me as a way of getting close to her. I didn't mind too much until one day in high school when the boy I was crushing on asked one of my friends out. I went home bawling, feeling super insecure about myself.

My mom came into my room to talk to me to see why I was so distraught. I shared with her that I wished I was as skinny and as pretty as my friends, even down to their perfect golden-glow skin tone. She taught me an important lesson that day that I will never forget. She said, "First of all, you are beautiful. And secondly, I want you to embrace your flaws, because those very things that you are insecure about will keep you modest and will protect you in your life."

As a fifteen-year-old, that is not what I wanted to hear. I thought she was so lame for saying that, and I was convinced she just didn't understand what I was going through—until I started to really let those words sink in, that is. Those same gorgeous friends experienced a lot more trials and temptations than I ever did. I quickly saw that I was actually living the life I wanted. It was okay that I wasn't perfect. My insecurities did in fact protect me. Mom was right!

The principle my mom shared with me that day has carried me through a lot in my life. The principle is that beauty comes from within. I love seeing women and men who are confident even though they may not be a cookie-cutter Barbie doll. I am not a Victoria's Secret model. Do I like to get dolled up? Yes! I love false eyelashes and makeup, but that is not my self-worth. All of the fluff has nothing to do with my true character or my self-worth. Body shape, name brands, and the latest trends aren't a person's real worth. Have you ever met someone who is not very attractive, yet they become so attractive because of their personality? Maybe you've experienced the reverse of that.

I have decided that I prefer to be attractive from the inside first. I know that I am a daughter of a loving Father in Heaven. That is my worth. I work on my inside. I meditate, I read scriptures, I listen to uplifting music. I sit in the quiet and try to receive the promptings that the Lord would have me know, and I try to act on those promptings in the very moment. I serve those around me and try to cheer up others. By writing this book, I pray that I can help *you* feel a bit better about yourself and your situation and give you the hope and the confidence to get back up and do your best **no matter what** that looks like to anyone else!

Charity

I believe that all people have certain gifts they are blessed with at birth. Sometimes it takes a lifetime to recognize those gifts and be able to claim our blessings. Some talents and their associated blessings are received only through hard work and practice. A musician or athlete may be blessed with natural ability, but if he does not work hard to practice his talent, he can ultimately lose it.

This has been my experience with charity. I have been blessed with an increased number of charitable qualities. But if I don't use and practice my gift of charity, then I will lose it.

As I recite my mantra and remember how I want to show up with charity each day, it has helped me make better decisions from a place of love and hope, even with some of the hardest decisions. For example, when I was supposed to drive the kids down to California for the weekend, I thought I was emotionally ready to go back to the city we called home for the previous ten years. But then I started to feel anxious and wondered if we should skip this trip. The problem with skipping the trip was that I didn't want to let Andy down. After all, I told him I would drive the kids down to see him this time.

I stopped and assessed my three core values. *What would "charity" do (charity with boundaries, that is)?* That includes having charity toward myself. So, I called Andy and told him that I felt I wasn't emotionally ready to be back in our hometown and see our home. I knew I would just yearn for the life we had. I was not trying to keep the kids away from him or add any more drama to this sad reality; I was simply trying to have charity and protect myself along the way.

Andy completely understood and booked a plane ticket, hotel, and rental car within fifteen minutes. How grateful I was that I was true and honest to myself and to Andy. I realize I am in a fragile state. I can have charity with boundaries!

I can have charity toward someone and disagree completely with that person. I can have charity toward someone else and have charity for myself at the same time. It is a tricky balance but one that is achievable. I am still learning how to find this balance.

Here's another example of charity that took place when Andy and I were working on our marriage. I have seen loved ones stay in an unhealthy marriage and hate every second of it. They resent and make negative gestures and comments toward each other at every opportunity.

I decided I didn't want to show up that way. I determined what charity would do, and then I acted accordingly. If I am choosing to stay, I decided, then I can choose my attitude. I tried each day to speak kindly (and I repented a lot of days too). I tried to think kindly of him. Perhaps that is why it was a shock to people when I announced to the world on social media that I was getting a divorce. Because I didn't wear our relationship hardships on my sleeve, I chose what was on my sleeve. I chose (for the most part) charity!

It takes a lot of work to show up in the attributes that mean the most to you. Be patient with yourself. But it sure is worth it for you and for your mental peace of mind.

You may be confused as to why I say that my definition of charity has boundaries when we so often hear how true love has no boundaries. Let me explain my perspective with this. We have laws that keep us safe—safe on the road, safe in our homes. The laws truly protect us. You may give a child a curfew not because you are mean and don't want her to have fun, but because there are boundaries that keep her safer than if she was to go and do whatever she wanted to at all hours of the night. In turn, if your child breaks curfew, do you love her less? No, but there are consequences and expectations.

I feel that this is also similar to the Ten Commandments that the Lord has set in place for us. Jesus has shown us the perfect example of how charity has boundaries. Does He love the sinner less? No, but we are rewarded for our actions accordingly.

So, when I show up as charity in my life, it means I love myself enough to have boundaries that keep me safe. It means I am not a pushover. I simply show up having charity for myself, and that includes having boundaries.

Hope

I learned about hope as a young child when I saw my single mom with no education, no job, and five kids. She showed me how a hope can turn into a reality. When you put your mind to your biggest dreams, you can make it all happen.

I am not in my ideal life right now at this moment. But what I do have is hope for a brighter time in life. Most people say a brighter tomorrow, but I think that it is going to take a bit longer than tomorrow to get me to where I hope to be. That's how it is with my life now. And that's how it is with your life. Wherever you are in life, you can put your chin up and smile intently and imagine your dream is coming true.

I have hope that my kids will be guided and protected through this crummy time in our lives. I have hope that I will continue to search and seek after the joy I long for. I have hope that one day Andy will understand what the Lord wants him to do with his life and make those necessary changes. I have hope that my businesses will take off and bless my family monetarily. I have hope that one day I will be with someone who shares my values and will be true and honest with me. Hope is a beautiful thing—even when I am ten feet underwater, I have hope that a lifesaver will be thrown to me just in time to pull me out and get me to shore!

You know what values I try to show up with and live by. Now it's your turn to dig deep and learn what values are most important to you and will help you live with no regrets from here on out. Forget your silly mistakes in the past; focus on this new roadmap with the intention for you to be your best self

No Matter What!

Whatever your circumstance is now, keep your new mantra always in the front of your mind as you intentionally make the next right decision, and then the next one, and then the next. Whether you have to tell yourself to focus on the good in your spouse or in your ex, like I have had to dig deep and do, my hope is that you feel more empowered and have more peace from within!

Deep Conversations with Coach Jamee

A key component to self-discovery that most people are unaware of is true self-compassion. Most people don't know what real self-compassion is. The true meaning of self-compassion is to support yourself through suffering. Developing the skill and ability to support yourself on your self-discovery path is extremely important. I learned true self-compassion from Danielle Savory, my personal coach who is near and dear to my heart.

Whenever you are doing this hard and deep work on yourself, lots of suffering can come up in the form of worry, a feeling of being overwhelmed, and possibly feelings of confusion and anger. You may even have thoughts that you are broken in some way. This is totally normal. However, without the self-compassion component, you can stay in your hurting or push it down, only to have it resurface later.

Self-compassion is the ability to recognize and offer understanding and support for your suffering. Self-compassion is the way in which you can support yourself and have your own back through the trial.

This support for yourself will enable you to create your own roadmap.

Self-compassion sounds like this: "Of course you are suffering; you are not at all where you imagined you would be," or, "Of course this is hard; you want something better for yourself." Here is an exact process that you can start implementing right now, no matter where you are and how you are feeling:

1.   Acknowledge Your Suffering

Start with **acknowledging whatever it is you are feeling,** whatever suffering you are experiencing. This is not an over-dramatization of your suffering. Examples of over-dramatization are thoughts like, *What is wrong with me? I am ruined!* Don't discount your suffering either by thinking things like, *I shouldn't be this sad,* or, *I actually have a lot to be grateful for, so I shouldn't be hurting.* I call this hitting yourself with a grateful stick. Without over-dramatizing or dismissing, acknowledge what you're feeling by thinking something like, *I'm hurting. Of course I am; I want something different for myself.* You're not trying to fix anything at this point; you're just trying to support.

2.   Connect to Yourself

Second, place your **hand on your heart** or hold your hands; you might also squeeze your arms as if you are giving yourself a hug. This skin-to-skin contact releases the brain hormone oxytocin, which is a nurturing hormone. When you stimulate the release of oxytocin, you are giving yourself what you truly need—nurturing and support.

3. Connect to Others

At this point, your brain will want to isolate you from others. This is normal, because we don't often talk about suffering in our culture. As a result, we believe we are alone in our suffering.

You might also tend to go down the road of "this isn't fair." The truth is, you are having a human experience. And all humans know what it feels like to hurt. You can simply offer words that connect you to the human race. Try something like, "All humans know what suffering feels like; I am not alone," and "All women have experienced anger or worry—this is normal."

4. Talk Kindly to Yourself

Last, **talk kindly to yourself,** as if you were a good friend. We tend to talk meanly to ourselves and say things that we would *never* say to a friend. Use kind, supporting, and encouraging words like, "You've got this," "I'm here for you," "We will figure this out," and "I'm learning."

As you practice self-compassion, you will nourish your soul and befriend yourself on this journey. You will clear out the judgments and the mean voices, and you will be able to think clearly and see your values. You will see that you are more capable than you realized and more understood than you imagined. You are worth the time and energy it takes to practice this skill. I promise that so much beauty and clarity are right around the corner for you.

Chapter 7

FIGHT FOR YOU!

Working on *you* is the first step to saving your marriage.

I think we all can agree that not every marriage can be saved. The only way to find out whether yours can be saved is to try, even when you do feel or perhaps know that the problems are not your fault. The magic happens when you take care of yourself!

Fighting for *you* is actually fighting for your marriage. Do I need to say that again? *Fighting for* you *is actually fighting for your marriage.* Fight hard. You are worth the fight! Your spouse will have to do work as well at some point to have a happy marriage. But starting with *you* is all *you* have control over! And love in your marriage starts with truly loving yourself.

If you love yourself hard enough, big enough, and bravely enough, you are all the love you will ever need! You can love yourself enough that you don't have to look for other people's approval or love. It truly doesn't matter if someone else loves you back. Learning this principle alone will save you a lot of stress, worry, anticipation, and even fear.

If you can honestly fill your own cup with love, you can stop searching for approval from other people. This is your chance to accept *you*. Accept your flaws. Accept that you are not perfect. No one is perfect—not one of the 7.6 billion people on earth right now is perfect. Why do you think you should be? So, start giving yourself some grace and just do YOU! When you pour more love into your own soul, you have that much more love to pour into the world. You cannot pour from an empty cup!

The first step toward achieving this love is accepting that this is one thing you *do* have control over. Throughout this entire book, we have discussed the fact that only *you* have control over yourself. You don't have control over anyone else's thoughts, boundaries, emotions, or actions. But you do have control over YOU! You get to have control over how you show up.

In this final chapter, I want to help you open your eyes and your heart and learn what it is that you need to do for *you*. I want to help give you more purpose so you can be intentional about how you are doing and how you are treating yourself.

This process looks different to every single one of us! But I am challenging you to show up as your best self and love *you* more. Let's look at a few ways to care for yourself physically, mentally, and spiritually.

Care for Yourself Physically

I believe that a lot of mental therapy happens when you physically put yourself first and learn to pamper yourself! My favorite days are when I allow myself to stop the mundane cycle of life and run and grab a yummy acai bowl on my way home from work. This simple thing is so therapeutic for me! It brings me joy. I don't do that every day, but on the days when I need an extra boost or love for myself, it is exactly what helps me feel better. I even find that a quick run into Marshalls or TJ Max to find a ten-dollar shirt is therapy! I challenge you to think about what brings you joy and stop waiting for someone else to deliver it to you. Take control and gift yourself! You deserve it!

What recharges you? Is it physically going out and getting into nature? Is it going on a weekend getaway with yourself? Is it hiring a house cleaner for a day? You get to decide!

I want you to think about your perfect day. What does it look like? What time do you wake up? What do you eat? Where do you go? What do you do? What do you think about? Picture your perfect day then ask yourself what is stopping you from doing at least one of those things today. You don't have to implement everything at once but knowing what brings you joy is powerful. Pull from this mental list when you are needing extra tender loving care.

Let's take this a step further. What if you were to set aside a certain amount of time just for you every single day? It might be ten minutes or two hours; that can vary. So can the time of day. But block this time out and fill that time with whatever makes you the happiest. Do whatever it takes to make this time special for you. Turn off your phone. Close and/or lock your bedroom door. Take a bath, meditate, get a pedicure, get your hair done, get a massage. Having **you** time will help **you** to feel more grounded. When I am more grounded, I find it so much easier to find joy amidst the chaos.

Care for Yourself Mentally

When someone asks you, "How are you?" your superficial answer might be, "Good." It's probably a habit; it is for most people. But in truth, there are a million thoughts and emotions racing through your head, and most often *good* is not even one of them. I have a close friend who calls me and makes me respond a second time to share exactly how I am really doing.

In somewhat the same way, I find that I often just superficially tell myself that I am good—even when I don't really believe it. But just like being a good friend means accepting people right where they're at, we can accept ourselves right where we are at. You are important. You are worth pausing to take a moment to care for yourself.

As I paused and evaluated how I was going to stay in my hard marriage and still find happiness from within, I realized I needed to do certain mental tasks to fuel myself and blossom into who I knew I wanted to be. I knew there were some things I needed to get rid of to clear my mind and stay positive and hopeful. I also knew that there were some things I needed to do more of.

I had an awesome business coach a few years ago who had me write down three things each week:

1. What went well?

2. What can I do more of?

3. What can I get rid of?

In business, you can often find yourself going down a deep rabbit hole, wasting mental energy, time, and money on things that aren't bringing you a return. But that's not restricted to business; it applies to everyday life as well.

This exercise was so therapeutic for me that I carried the concept into my personal life. Each Sunday I reevaluate by asking myself, *What can I do more of? What can I eliminate to help me be my better self and love myself more deeply?* Here is what my personal list looked like one week. Hopefully it will spark a chord with you and help you decide how you can love yourself more!

What can I do more of:

Pause and evaluate

Treat myself

Serve my soul

Read the scriptures

Pray more intently

Look for ways to serve others

Things I need to get rid of:

Negative thoughts

Revengeful thoughts

Falling into a victim role

Songs, movies, tv shows that trigger me

Certain friends

Being on social media too long

I had to change things that I thought I really enjoyed. But at the end of the day, those were the things that left me with a lot of sadness, extra worry, and unnecessary heartache. For example, watching *The Bachelor* is so fun, but I could see that after watching it, I was not in a good place mentally. It was a bad kind of trigger. I chose to give up watching it, and when I did, I found those triggers were not as strong. (I will take any relief I can get when it comes to staying strong and protecting myself.) Now, if you are a person who loves to watch *The Bachelor*, there is absolutely no judgment here.

This was my own refining process. I call it survival. I call it me trying not to fall off the cliff I am teetering over! Just like you, I have control only over my thoughts and my actions. If I want to show up as my best self, I have to make sacrifices, be intentional, treat myself with love, and remember to pamper myself in the process.

Care for Yourself Spiritually

Regardless of your faith or formal church membership, taking care of your spiritual soul is essential. Whether you channel your inner core with the universe or you find yourself in humble prayer and scripture, having a higher power to reach toward when times are rough is essential for survival and success.

As I chose to stay in my hard marriage, I knew I wanted to stay with joy. I didn't want bitter feelings. I didn't want to feel like I was the victim. In order to thrive where I was, I learned that I am sensitive to wholesome and encouraging things in my life. I had to read more scriptures. I read because I am desperately pleading for the Lord to bless me with strength—strength to not shrivel up in a ball and never leave my room. Strength and courage to follow the promptings of the Spirit. Strength to endure the hardest trial of my life. I needed blessings. I could not afford to not read my scriptures.

When I read my scriptures, I literally have to stop my life—stop my brain from being sidetracked. I plead for the Lord to bless me with clarity for my life as I give Him some time, whether that is five minutes or fifty minutes. I literally pray and tell Him, "Okay, Heavenly Father, this is your time. If there is something you need me to know right now, please make it known. I'm listening and ready to hear and act on the promptings you have for me today."

I chose to create that habit, and I have to choose every day to continue the habit. It's not an easy choice. It is so much easier to **not** read scriptures, or serve someone else, or go to church, or help the gluten-free community, or feed my children every ten minutes! But I do it. I call it survival. I call it taking time to love myself through the Great Creator.

Taking time for my Creator is not easy for me. Someone once told me, "I wish reading the scriptures regularly came **naturally** to me like it does for you." I was absolutely shocked. Daily scripture study does *not* come easily for me at all. We all have the same number of hours in the day. At the time this was said to me, I was working outside of the home, had a demanding leadership position serving the women at church (as the stake Relief Society president), and was trying to keep my head and heart sane enough to save my marriage. I was doing all that while trying to be the best mom I could be. And she thought that scripture study came easily for me?!

Even though taking this time can be difficult, the Lord always makes it worth my while. One of my favorite church hymns of all times is, "I Know That My Redeemer Lives." Verse three starts out, "He lives, my kind, wise heavenly Friend." These seven words pierce my soul and give me so much comfort. I have a God, a Heavenly Friend, who wants to help me, who loves me, who knows me. He gives me strength. So, when I need to love myself more, I turn to the Maker who loves me the most. He gives me the strength and courage to fight for me. After all, He suffered so that I personally may find true joy and have everlasting happiness. So yes, self-evaluating my relationship with Him is crucial for me personally. Reading my scriptures and tuning into my spiritual needs allows me to show up as my best self.

This spiritual fine-tuning reminds me that *I* get to decide how I show up. I wanted to show up and fight for my marriage. I knew that I would have regrets if I didn't fight hard for it. If I can weed out the things that trigger me, **no matter what** they are, I am so much better off! I am here trying to be my best self while loving myself enough to stay and **fight** for the marriage I signed up to **fight** for!

Deep Conversations with Coach Jamee

I hear a lot of women say that they feel terrible because they don't even know what they like to do, how to really care for themselves, and what nourishes their souls. I hear women say that they are a *grown woman* and should know exactly what they need to feel loved and cared for. I also hear women say that they have absolutely no time for themselves. If this sounds like you, I want you to pause right now and just take a deep breath.

The truth is that you shouldn't know what you need to feel loved and well taken care of. Why? Because first, there isn't a class we all take that teaches us exactly what we need, and second, we have been taught that as women we should be giving, giving, giving of our time and selves to everyone else. We have been taught to say no to ourselves and yes to everyone else. We have been taught that saying yes to ourselves is selfish and mean. And then we have been taught to be accommodating to everyone else. We've been told that accommodating others is better than saying yes to ourselves. These are just lies.

So, I invite you to do is put your hand on your heart and take a deep breath. You are exactly who you are supposed to be at this moment. There is absolutely nothing wrong with you. The first step to loving you and finding out what you need as an individual woman and to feel loved and nourished is to be able to offer yourself understanding, support, and true self-compassion. You will be able to fight for yourself when you make the decision to say yes to you in so many ways.

Parting Thoughts

Friends, in closing this book, I have a lot of emotions. But mostly, I don't really want it to end! I feel like this has been one of the most therapeutic accomplishments of my life. I never in my wildest dreams thought that *I* would write a book. I am sure it will be a great surprise for every English professor I ever had as well!

But ultimately, I hope I have empowered you with tools to fight for your marriage and to fight for *you*. I hope you're able to create a roadmap that will enable you, from here on out, to live a life with few to no regrets. I envision you being able to love your children and help them through these tough times. I can see you in my mind's eye, establishing clear boundaries with what feels morally right for you! And as I sit in all the emotions of this book coming to an end, I'm hoping you will realize every emotion is useful and needed for you to heal.

I want to end with an excerpt that I wrote about a month ago in my journal on a rainy Friday night that I feel sums up my message. I should also remind you that you are not alone in this uncertain and tough time. You and me, we are going to be just fine —

No Matter What!

This is the first weekend Andy has the kids. I am so sad. The kids got loaded up in the car, and I just bawled. The kids couldn't see me. But Andy came back in to ask a quick question and saw me in my distressed state. He looked at me and helplessly asked if I needed a hug. I said no, then I said yes, and we embraced. It wasn't a butterfly kind of hug, nothing like "I want you back." It was an "I am sad and thank you for understanding" hug.

I cried most of the afternoon. Took a nap. I was able to embrace the fact that this is sad. A dear friend called me. We chatted and cried together, we even laughed a lot — really, how else do you get through the crappy in life? Now, I am back to typing away on the computer. Crying. Typing and eating my gluten-free, dairy-free, microwavable burrito on a Friday night. As crazy as this is, I am realizing this is exactly where I need to be right now at this moment. It is hard, but it is also empowering. Because I have been true to myself and God, I am going to be just fine —

No Matter What!

NOTES

Made in the USA
Columbia, SC
19 May 2021